ANSWER ME THIS, WORLD BOOK

Is the Milky Way made out of milk?

World Book
answers YOUR questions
- about -
outer space

WORLD BOOK

www.worldbook.com

The questions in this book came from curious kids just like you who want to make sense of the world. They wrote to us at World Book with nothing but a question and a dream that the question they've agonized over would finally be answered.

Some questions made us laugh. Others made us cry. And a few made us question absolutely everything we've ever known. No matter the responses they induced, all the questions were good questions.

There isn't a strict rule for what makes a question good. But asking any question means that you want to learn and to understand. And both of those things are very good.

Adults are always asking, "What did you learn at school today?" Instead, we think they should be asking, **"Did you ask a good question today?"**

How far up there

is space?

Space begins beyond 50 miles (80 kilometers) above Earth's surface. That doesn't seem that far, right? It's just the distance from Long Island to New York City. Or from Chicago to...50 miles outside of Chicago. The distance between is called the atmosphere. The atmosphere is a mass of gasses that surrounds the entire planet.

What are shooting stars?

You were probably told to wish upon a shooting star.

Your wish may have been, "I wish someone tells me what a shooting star is." Well, your wish came true. A shooting star is a meteoroid that burns up as it moves through Earth's atmosphere. A meteoroid comes in many different sizes. It can be as small as a grain of sand or as big as a boulder. So shooting stars are not actually stars. But we still think you can wish on them.

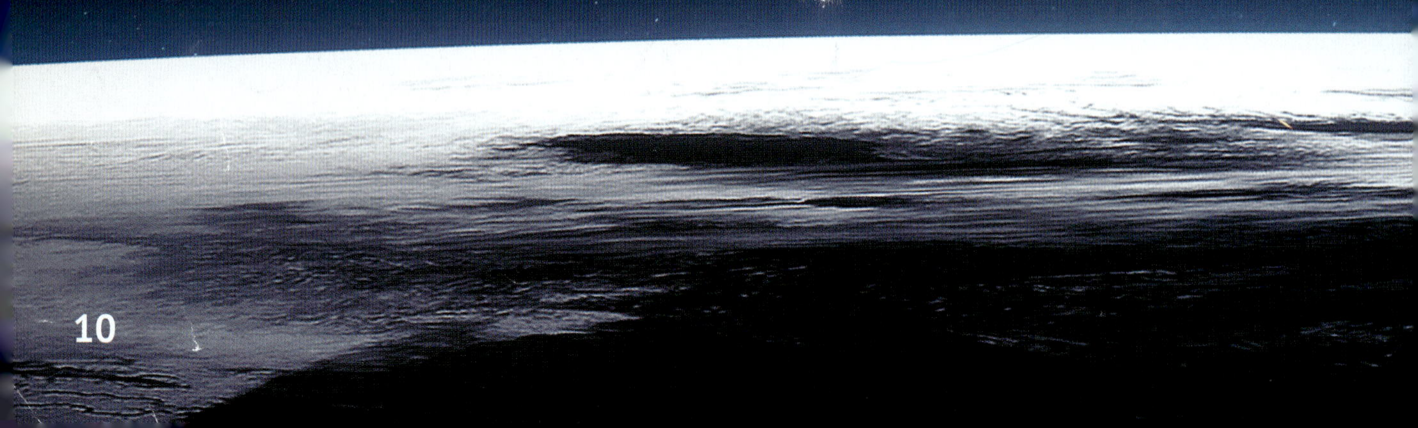

Why haven't astronauts

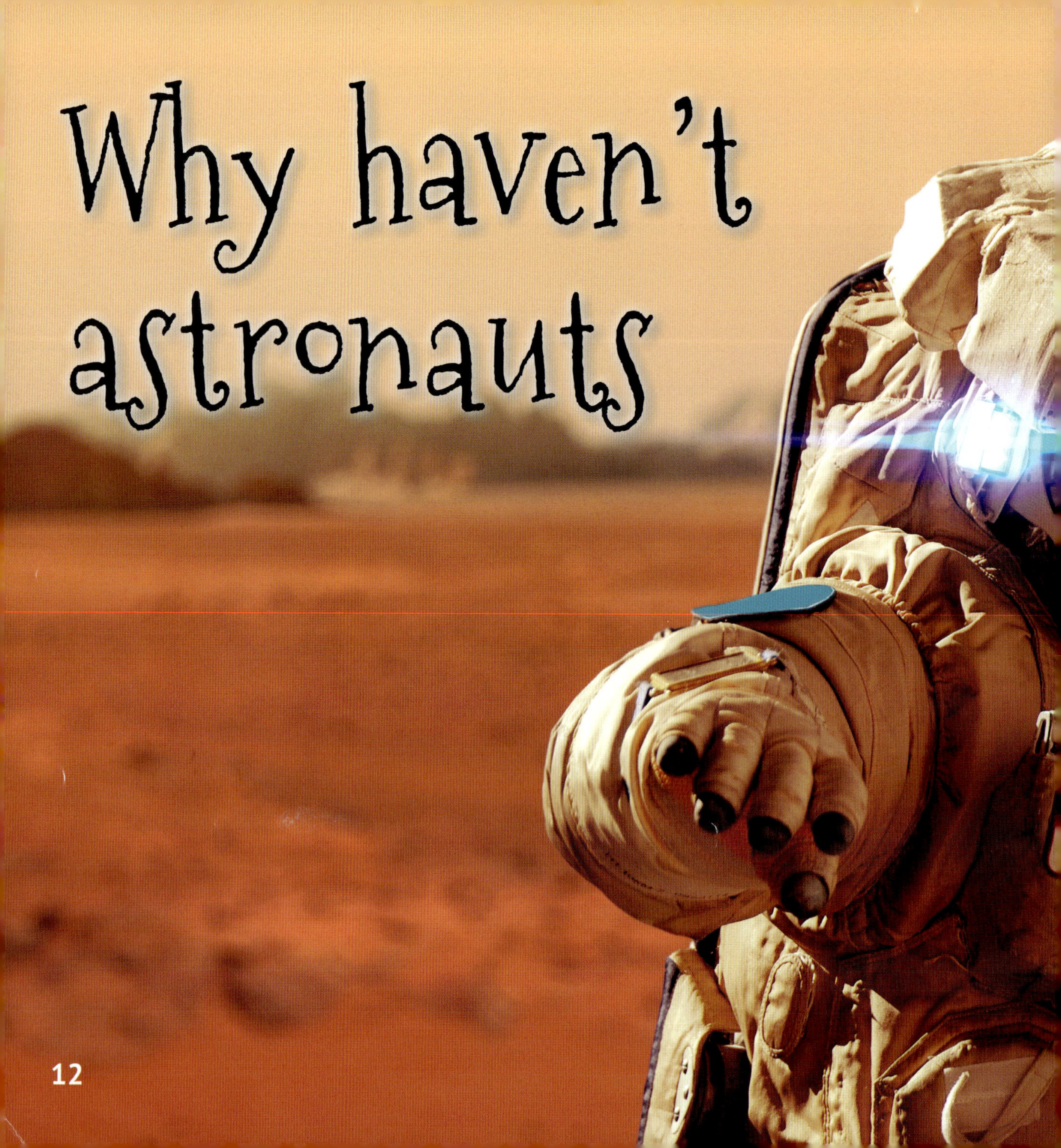

traveled to Mars?

Have you ever been on a reaaaaaally long road trip?

Maybe you went on one once, and your little sister wouldn't be quiet, and your older brother kept playing his music too loudly, and you got really sore sitting in the seat for all those hours. A trip to Mars would be like that for astronauts…except it would take about six whole months. Plus, that much time in a spacecraft has a lot of risks: they're too far from Earth to return if something goes wrong, they risk encountering too much radiation from the sun, and their bones and muscles would waste away from all that time with no gravity.

Why do things float in space

and not
on Earth?

You know how when you drop your ice cream, it falls straight to the ground?

That's gravity—a force that pulls toward the center of our planet. Every planet has its own gravity, though they're often quite different than Earth's gravitational pull. In space, far from the planets, gravity seems to barely act on objects. It's called *microgravity* (*micro-* means small, tiny, itty-bitty). But here on Earth, gravity is keeping us in our places.

How long will the sun burn?

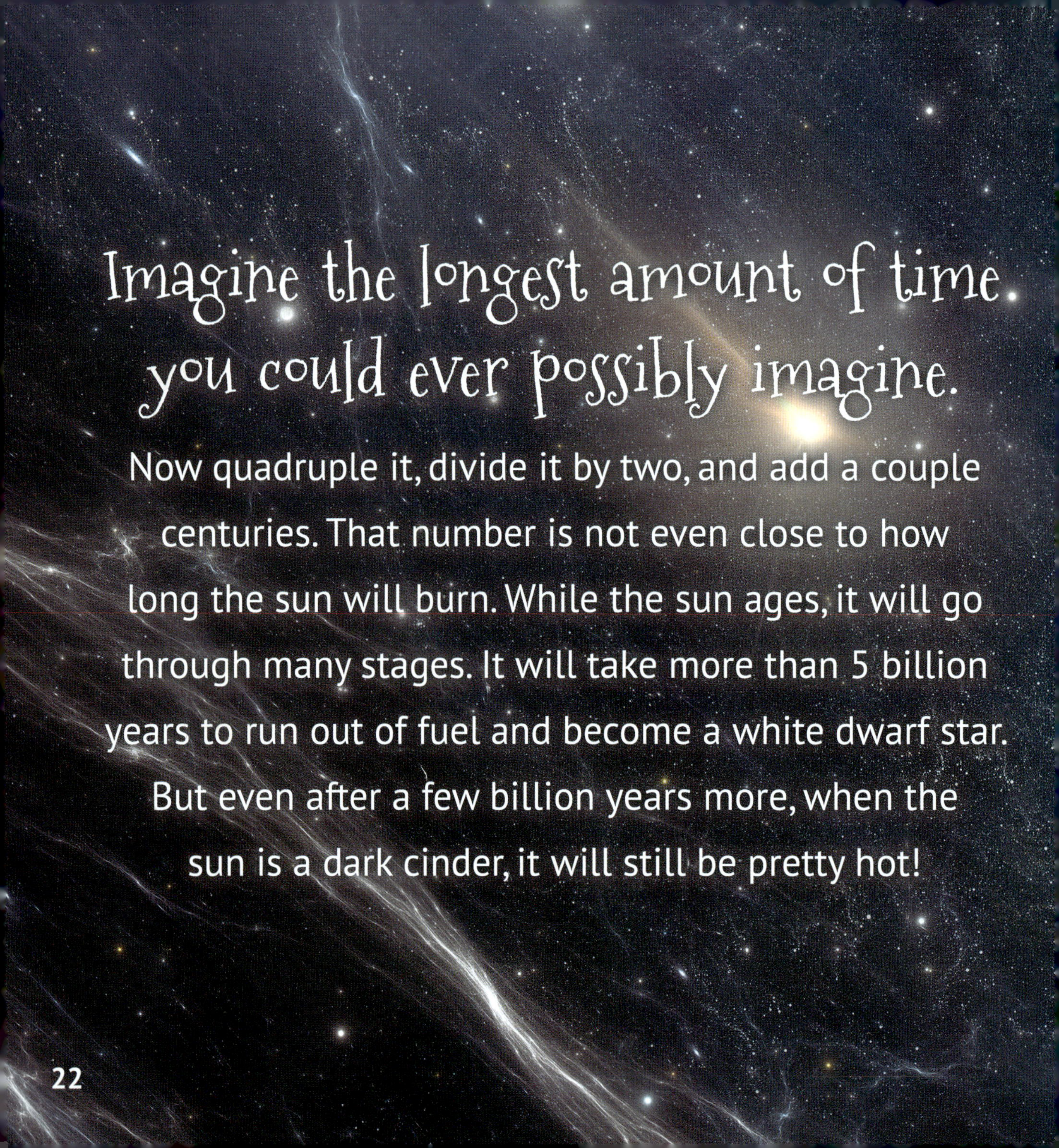

Imagine the longest amount of time you could ever possibly imagine.

Now quadruple it, divide it by two, and add a couple centuries. That number is not even close to how long the sun will burn. While the sun ages, it will go through many stages. It will take more than 5 billion years to run out of fuel and become a white dwarf star. But even after a few billion years more, when the sun is a dark cinder, it will still be pretty hot!

What would happen to Earth if all of the planets disappeared?

Earth would be pretty bummed. But it would probably continue orbiting uninterrupted. It would just revolve with a little less oomph. It would especially miss Jupiter. They have a complicated relationship. Scientists who study them from afar can't decide. Does Jupiter shield Earth from deadly asteroid and comet impacts with its powerful gravitational pull, making it safer for life? Or does its massive size dislodge comets and asteroids and shower them down on Earth? They can't decide. Maybe they're frenemies.

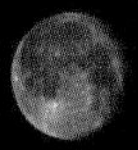

How hot can the sun be?

The sun is so hot that you could bake cookies on it.

But the cookies would burn instantly. While most cookie recipes call for a baking temperature of 375 °F (190 °C), the temperature of the sun is hotter than that. Much hotter. The part of the sun that we see has a temperature of about 10,000 °F (5500 °C). In the sun's core, temperatures can exceed 27 million °F (15 million °C).

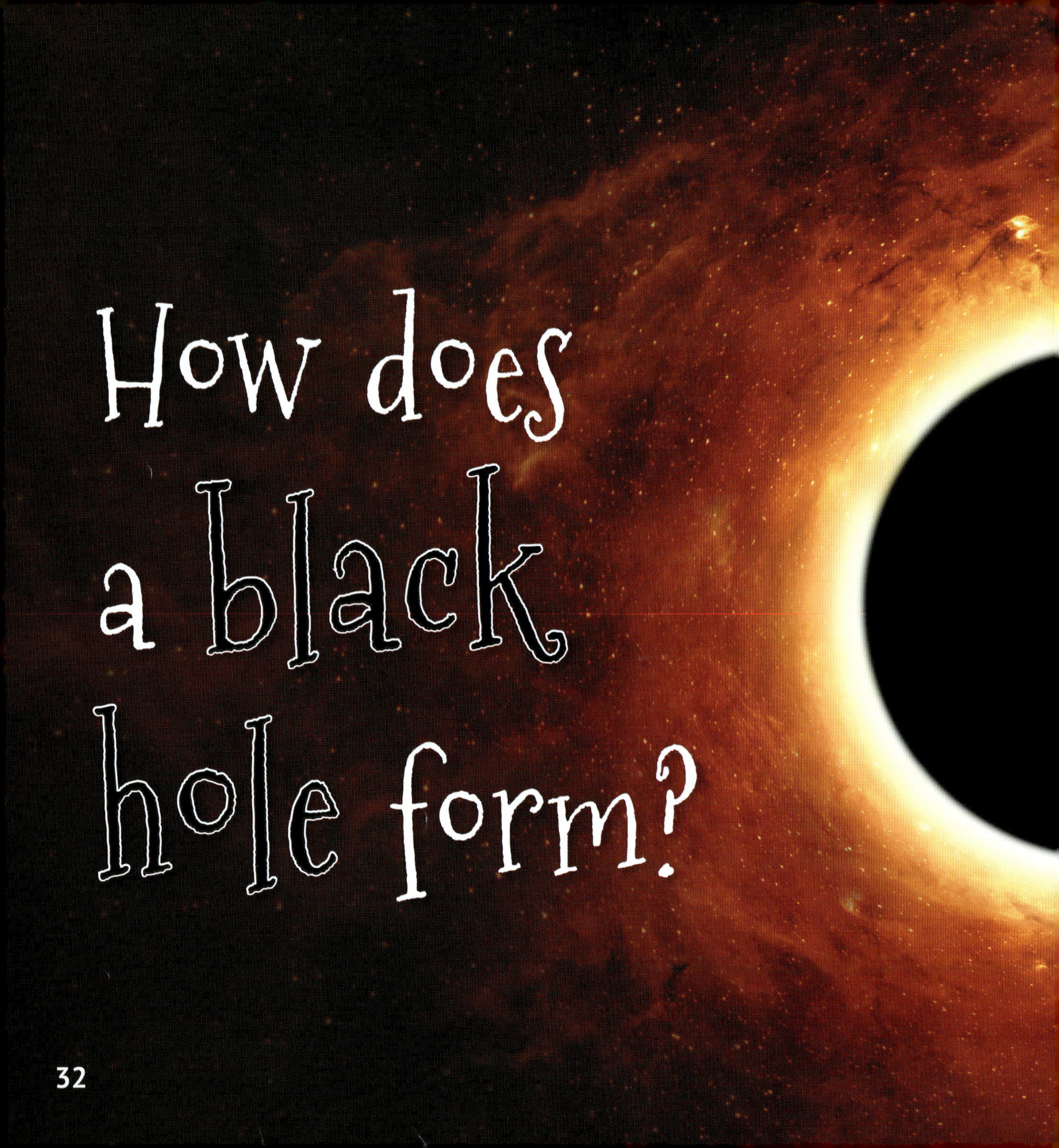

How does a black hole form?

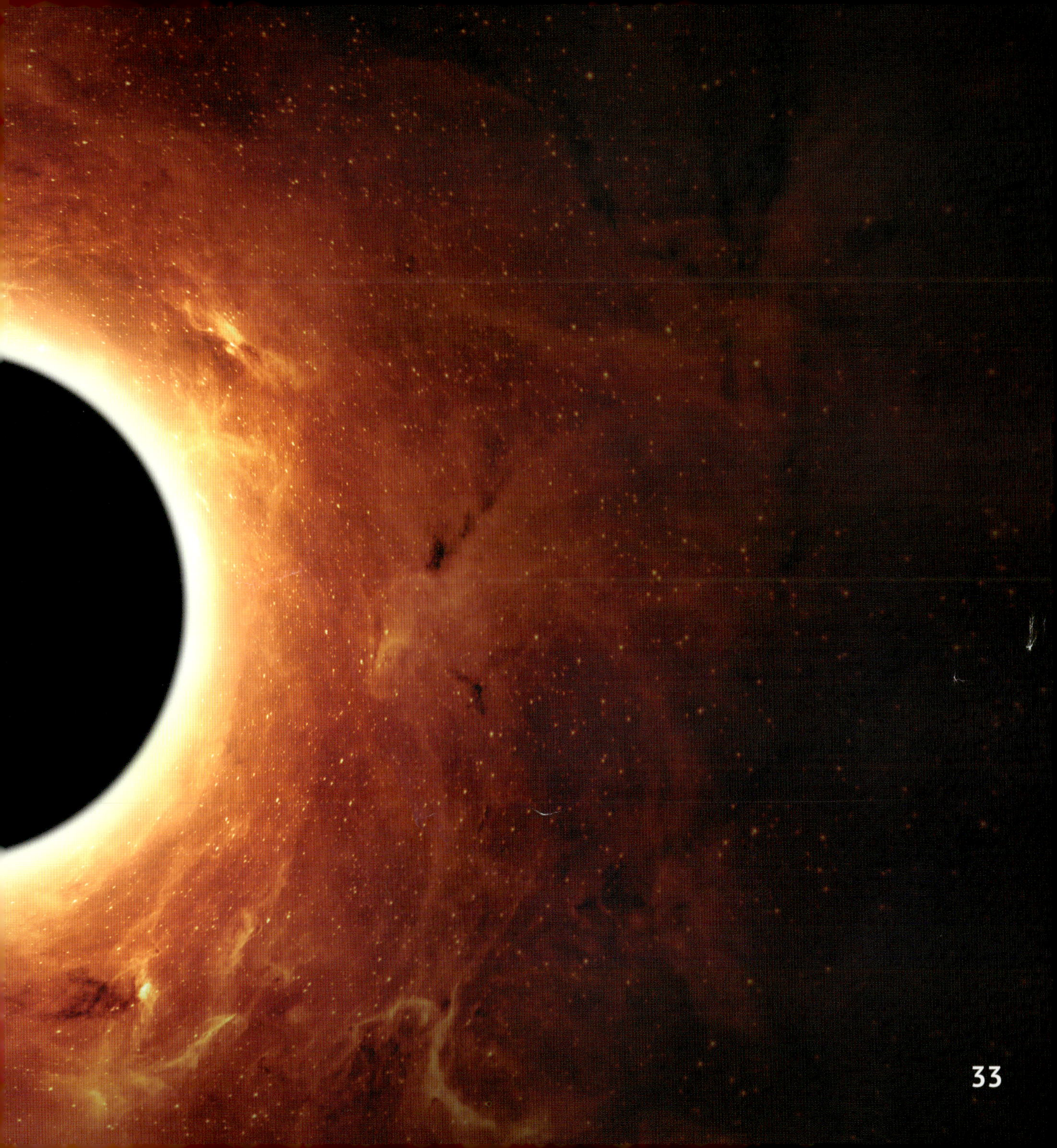

It's actually kinda sad.

A black hole is an area of space whose gravitational force is so strong and powerful that nothing can escape from it. Here's where the sad part comes in: a black hole forms when a giant star dies. (sniffle) When a really, really, really big star runs out of fuel, the outer layers collapse. Then there's a huge explosion called a supernova and the star collapses into a black hole.

What is a light-year?

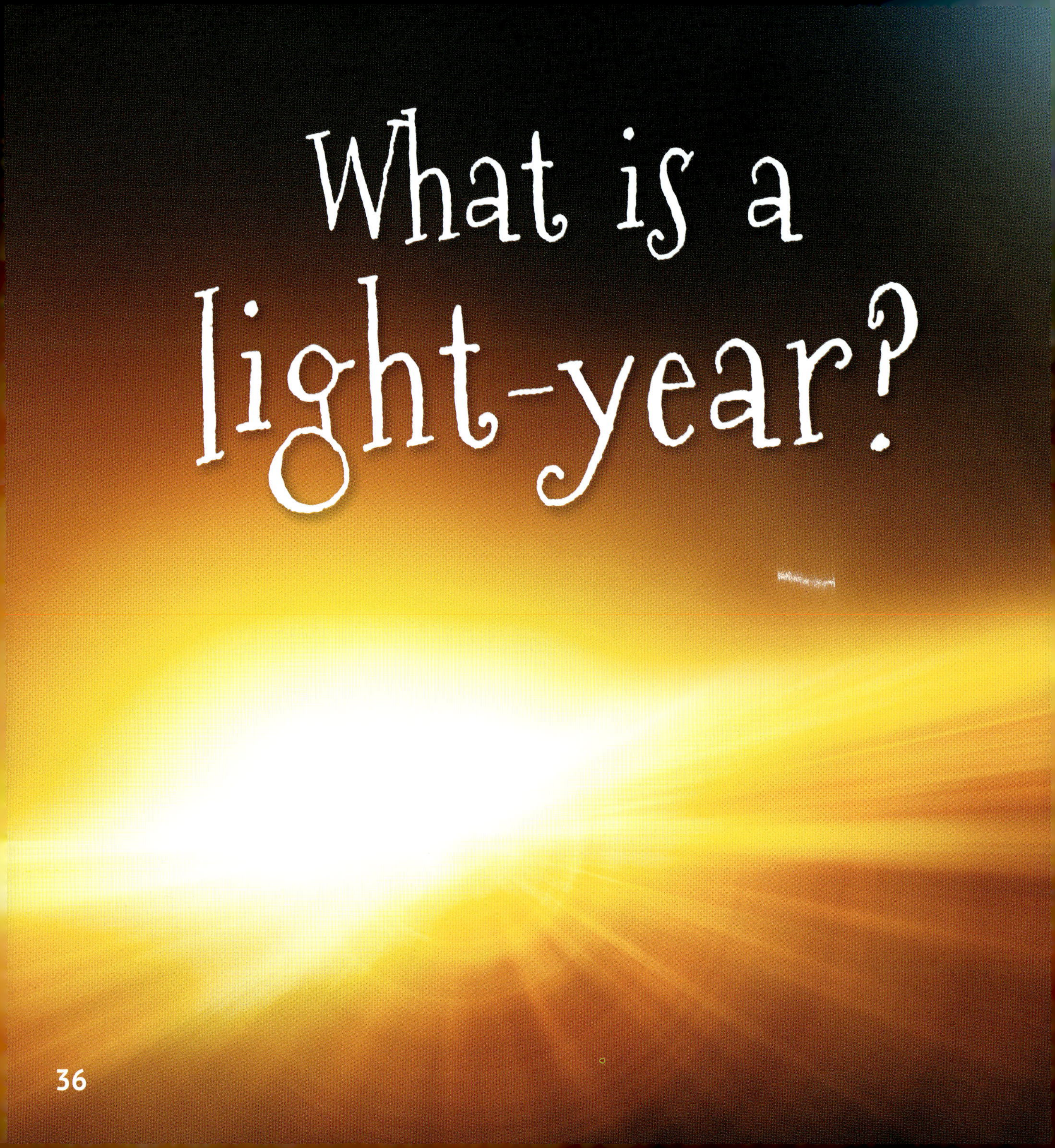

A light-year does not mean a year in which you have a lot of free time.

It is the distance traveled in one year by a pulse of light. Light travels at 186,282 miles (299,792 kilometers) per second. One light-year equals about 5.88 trillion miles (9.46 trillion kilometers).

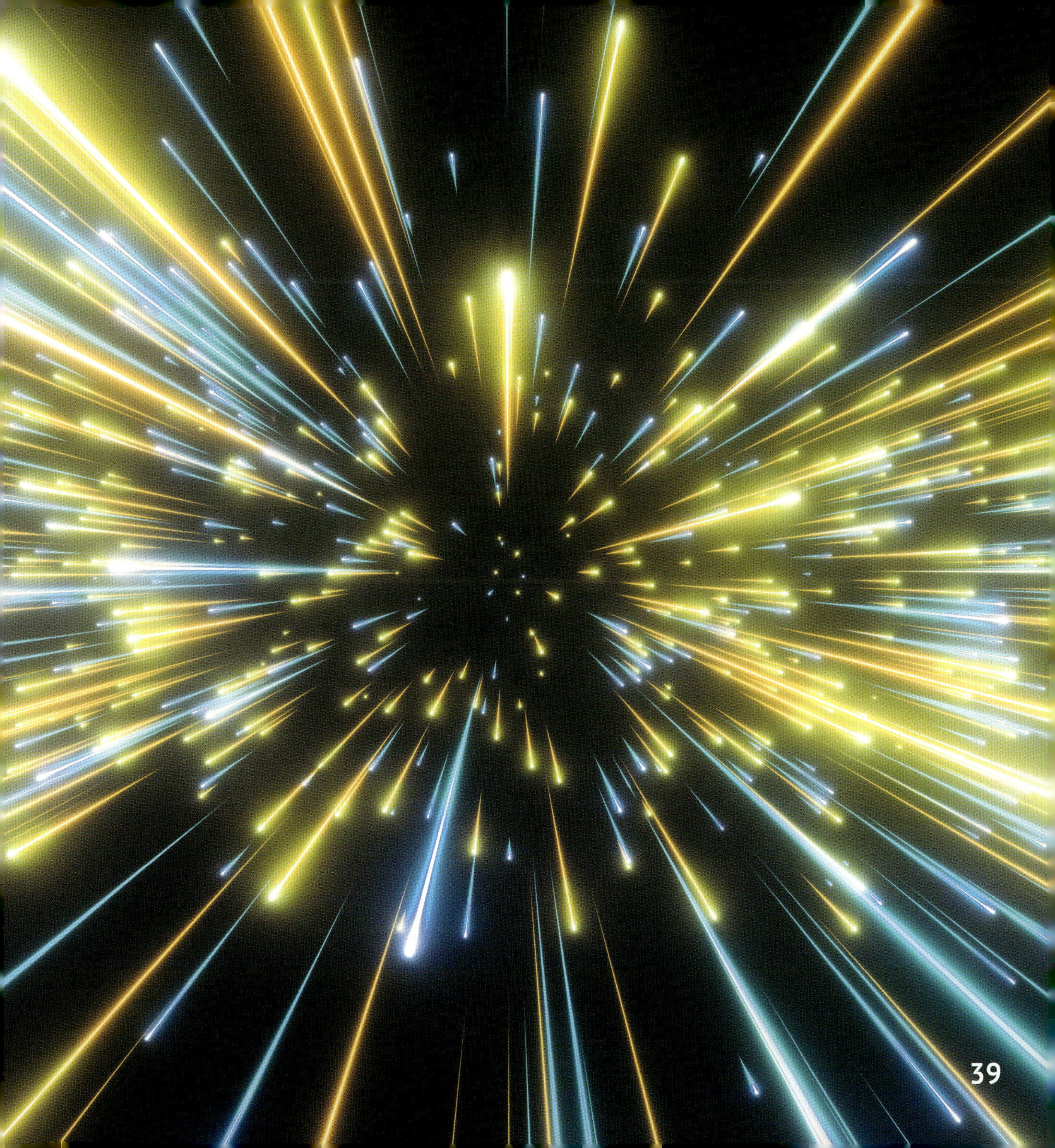

Why is Mars red?

It's feeling better!

It used to have the blues, meaning it used to be sad. And Mars is feeling red rather than blue because of its fine-grained reddish dust. The dust has a lot of iron oxide (rust). It covers the whole surface. And puts Mars in a better mood.

Why do the moons of other planets have names, but our moon is just called "the moon"?

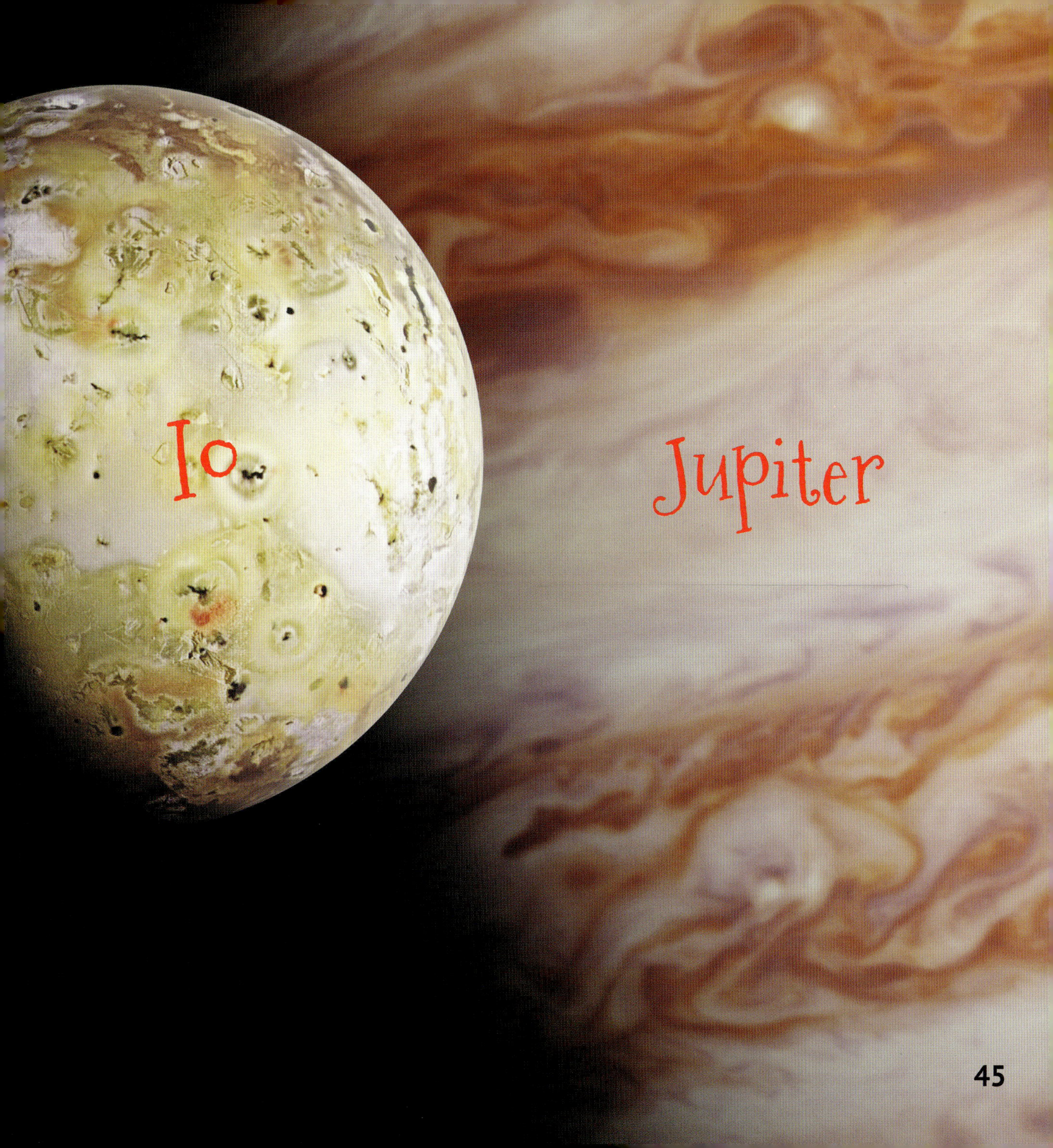
Io
Jupiter

Because it was the first.

Well, in terms of discovery. People didn't know other moons existed until 1610. That's when Galileo Galilei first saw Jupiter's moons. Plus, the "moon" is only the English name. In Latin and Spanish, it's "luna." In Swahili, it's "mwezi."

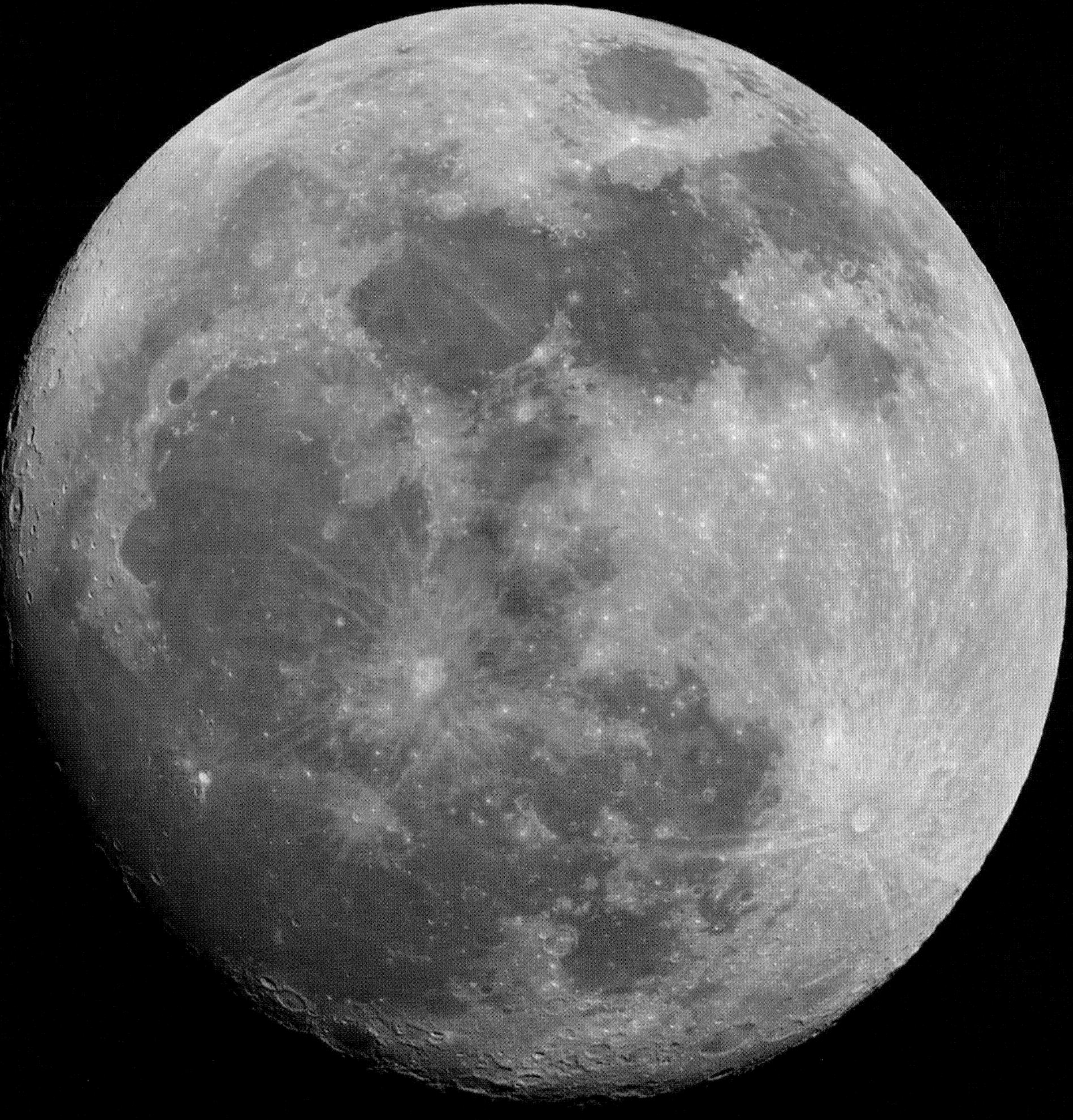

How far apart

are the stars?

Ya know how on your long ride your little sister kept asking, "Are we there yet?"

Well, she'd have to ask that many, many, *many* times if she was between the stars. The nearest star to Earth is the sun. And that's 93 million miles (150 million kilometers) from Earth. The closest star to the sun is about 4.2 light-years from the sun and Earth. One light-year equals about 5.88 trillion miles (9.46 trillion kilometers). So, no, you would not be "there yet" for a very long time. You better go the bathroom at the next rest stop.

If Earth was square, would there be any difference?

Yes.

Earth would be very different, like so different you wouldn't even believe it. Earth is round because of its gravity. And Earth's gravity also holds people and other bodies to its surface. So, if Earth was square, that would mean there wasn't any gravity. Which means we'd fly off the face of Earth. So, yes, there would be a difference.

How big is

the sun?

The sun's radius

(distance from its center to its surface) is as big as trillions of marbles, thousands of football fields, hundreds of whales, and one limousine. That turns out to be about 432,000 miles (695,500 kilometers). That's approximately 109 times Earth's radius. It was 108.5 times Earth's radius, but that limousine pushed it over the edge.

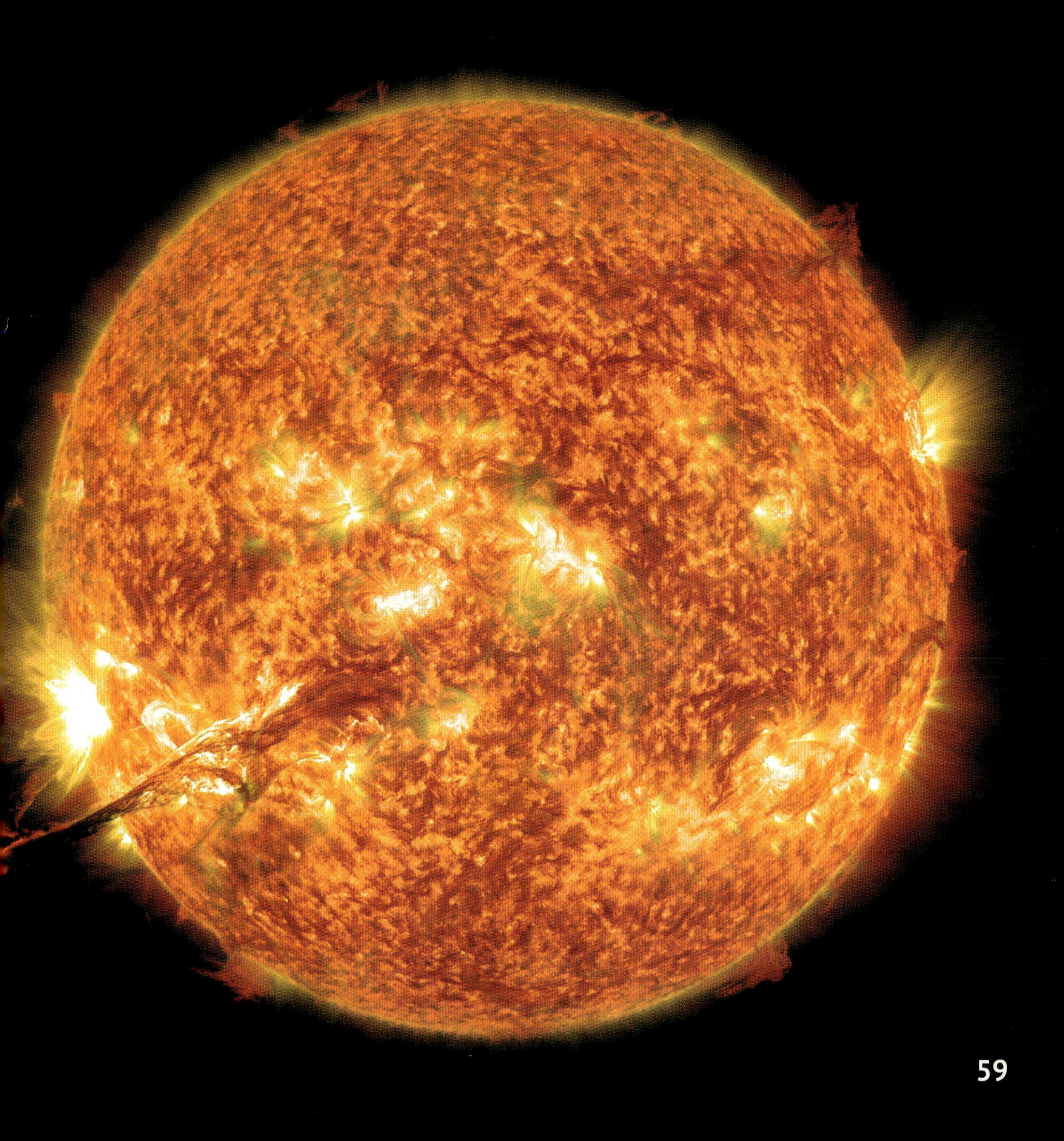

Is our galaxy endless space?

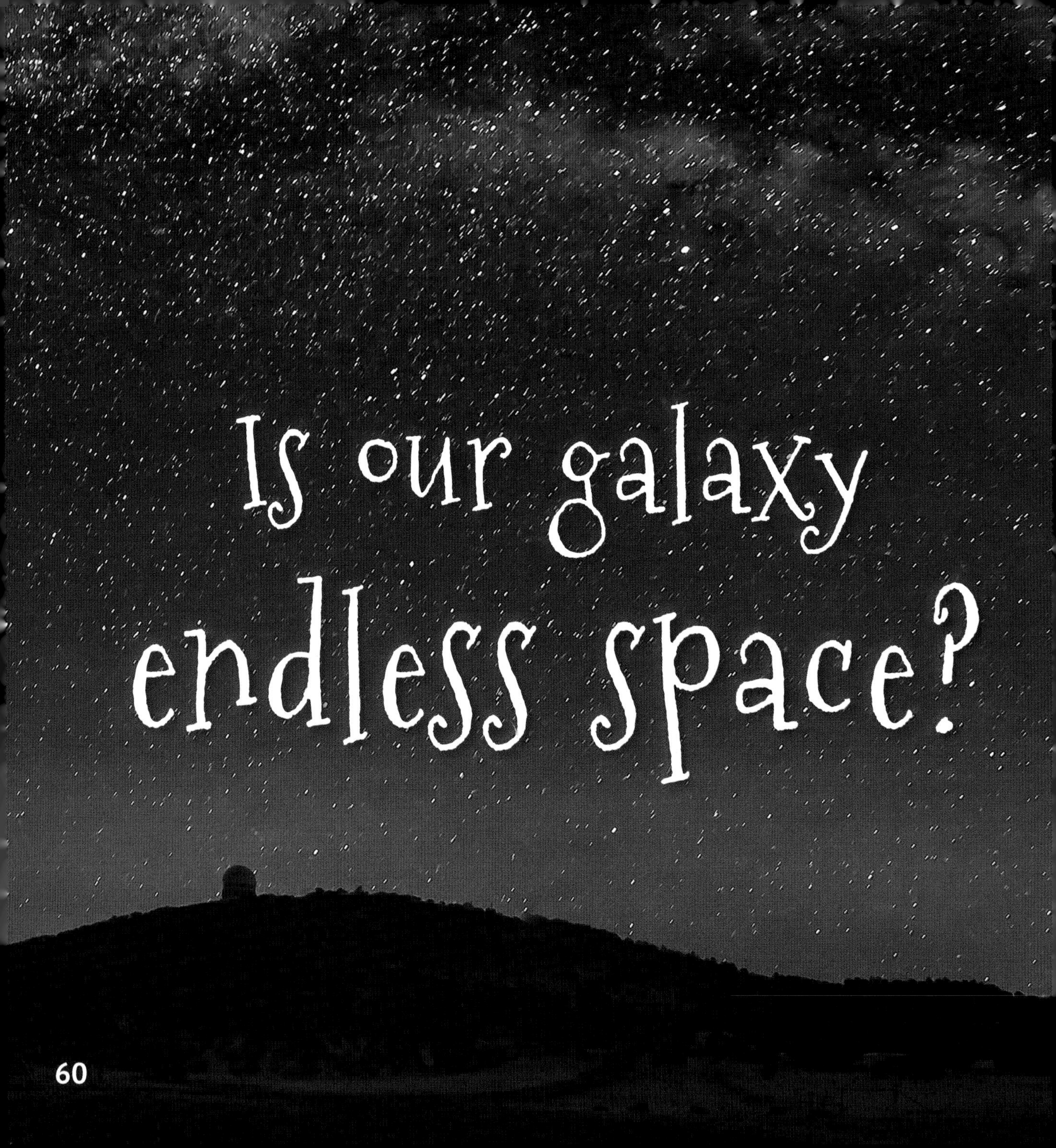

We don't know about endless,

but there sure are millions and millions of miles of it. A galaxy is a large system of stars, gas, dust, and other matter held together by gravity.

Our galaxy is the Milky Way. Some astronomers think that the size of the Milky Way is about one trillion times that of the sun.

Is the Milky Way made out of milk?

Yes. And planets are cookies.

Mars is chocolate chip and Venus is red velvet. Jupiter was a baking experiment gone awry. They tried to lasso a candy cane around a peanut butter cookie. Just kidding! The huge, milky band you see is actually the light of billions of faraway stars that are part of our galaxy. The milky glow inspired the name.

Could there be other living beings in space?

G7

Maybe. And scientists are working really hard to solidify an answer. It's possible that Mars could have had life forms. But that would've been billions of years ago. Scientists are also exploring if a moon of Jupiter called Europa and a moon of Saturn called Enceladus could have life. With probably hundreds of billions of other planets in our galaxy alone, the odds suggest that life emerged somewhere else out there.

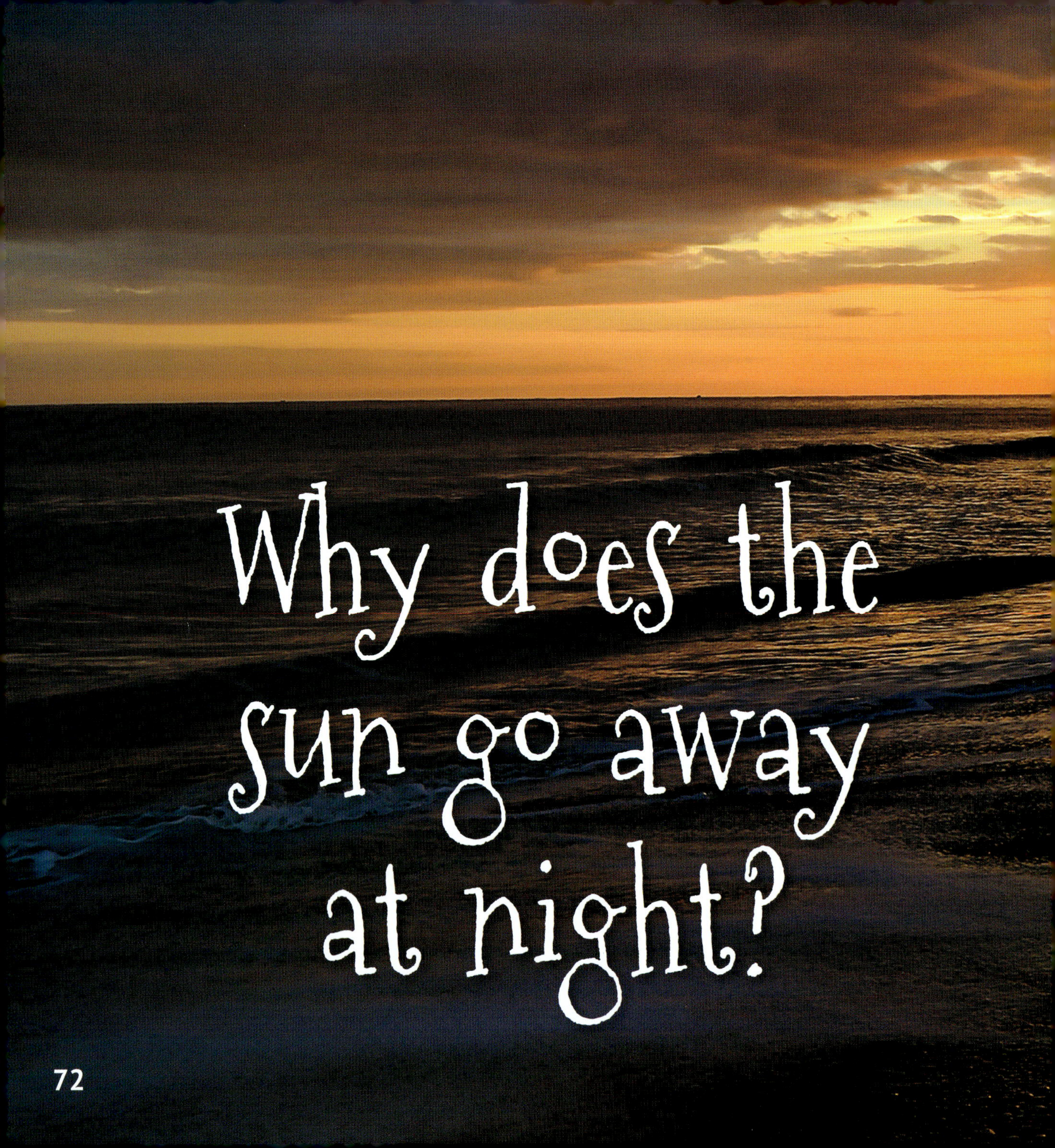

Why does the sun go away at night?

It might seem like the sun goes away at night,

but actually, you are going away. Imagine it's just after 12 o'clock noon. As Earth spins on its axis, the spot you're standing on spins away from the sun. As Earth keeps spinning, it brings you back to the sun. Do you know how you can tell you are back with the sun? You can see the sunrise!

Why are planets named after characters in Greek mythology?

Easy answer: they aren't.

Planets are named after characters in Roman mythology. Jupiter was named after the king of the Roman gods: Jupiter. Mars was named after the god of war: Mars. Mercury was named after the messenger of the gods: Neptune. Just kidding, we wanted to see if you were paying attention.

Jupiter

Neptune

Mercury

Venus

Mars

How do lunar and solar eclipses occur?

Location, location, location.

Eclipses occur when the sun and the moon are in such a location that they are in each other's way. A lunar eclipse occurs when the moon passes through Earth's shadow. A solar eclipse occurs when Earth passes through the moon's shadow. The moon blots out the sun, shrouding the affected region in a midday twilight. If you are in a location where you can see a solar eclipse occur, be sure to wear protective eyewear. Fun fact: we used the word "location" five times in that paragraph. Six if you count the fun fact.

LUNAR ECLIPSE

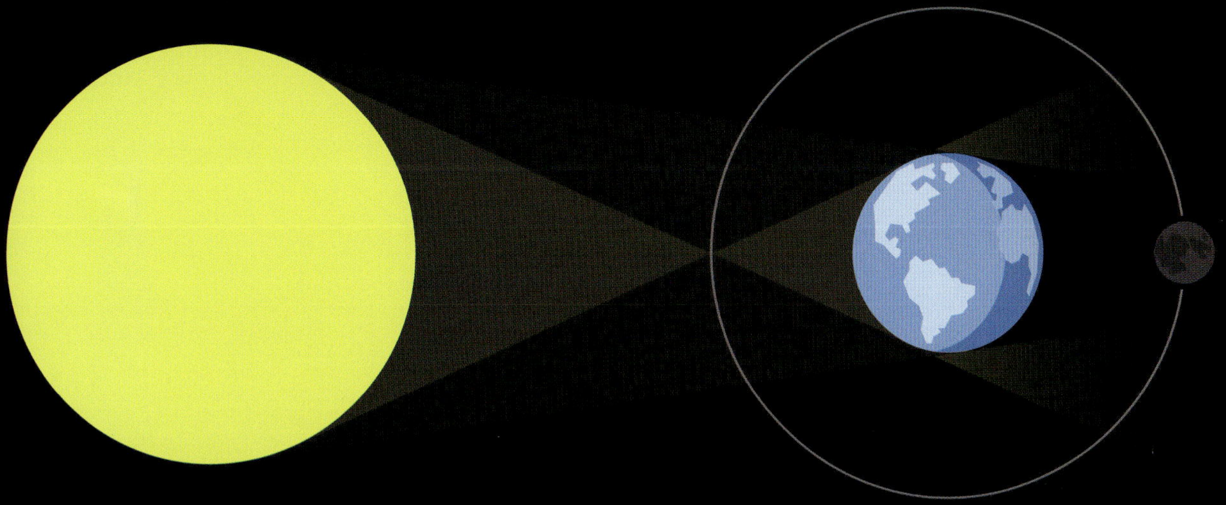

SOLAR ECLIPSE

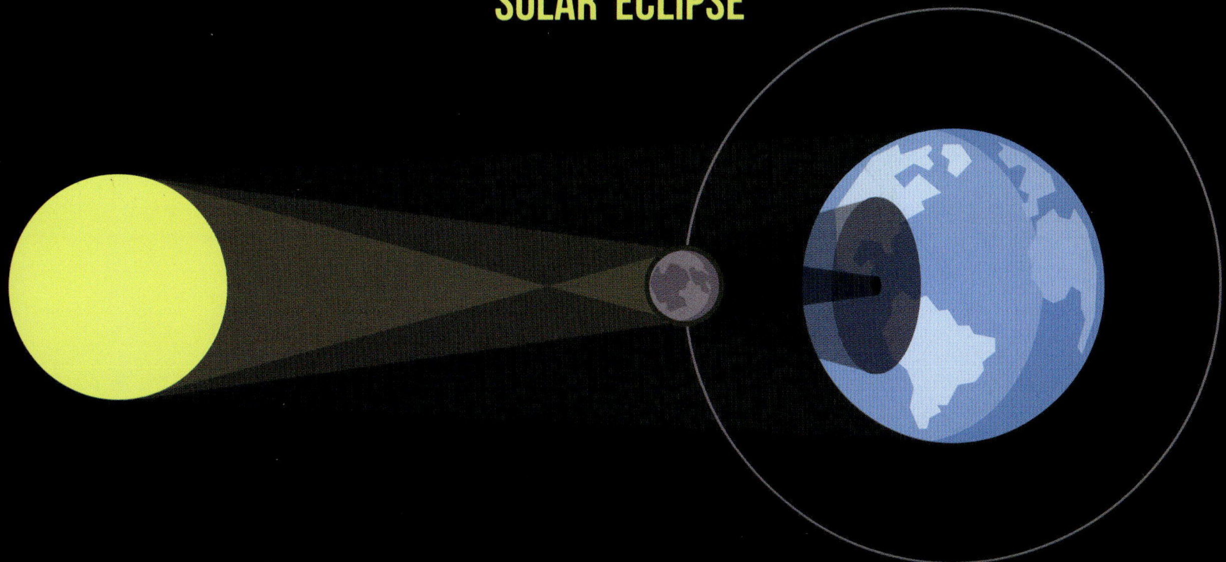

If Earth is orbiting the sun so fast, then why can't we feel it, and why aren't we getting blown off the planet?

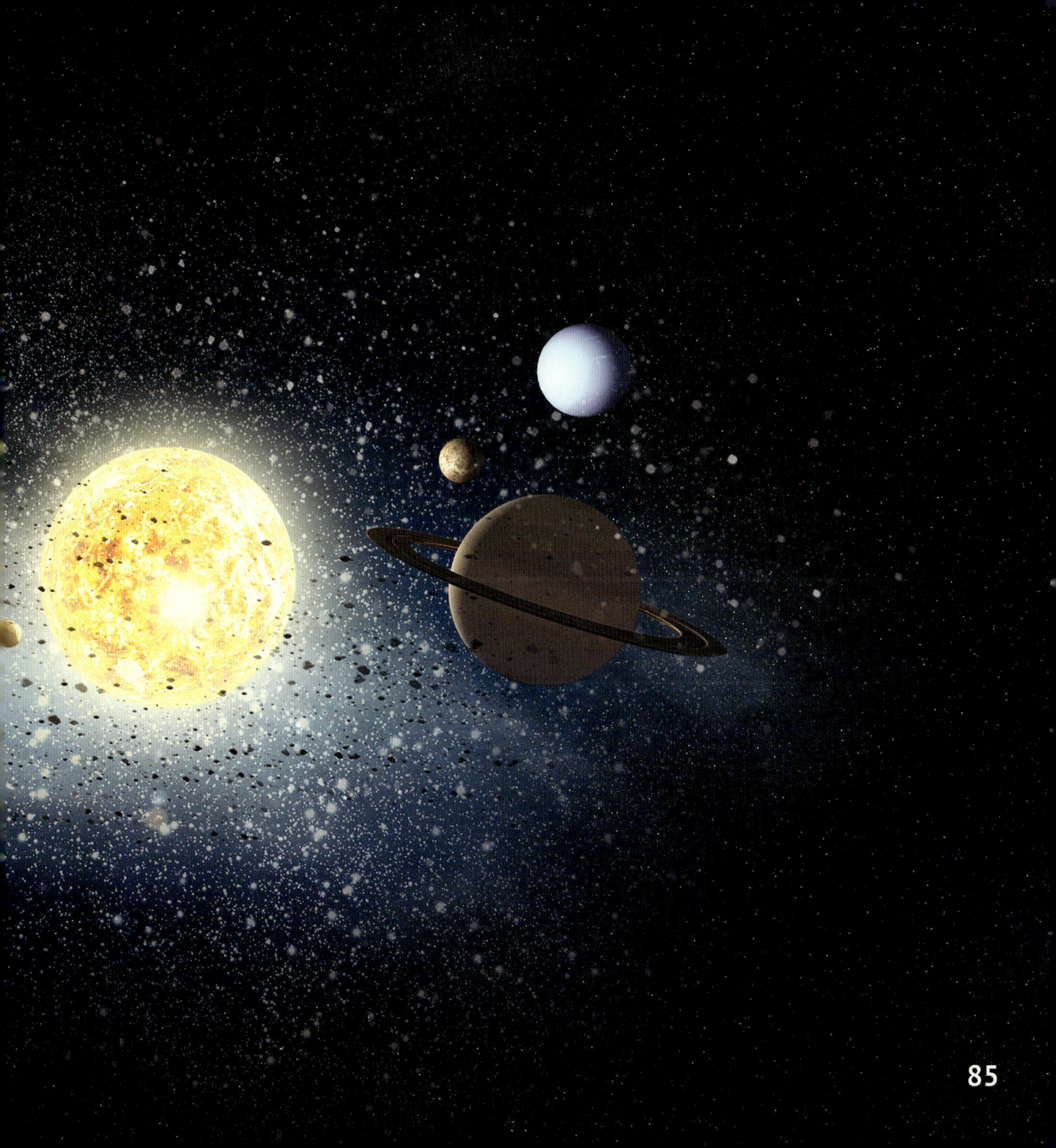

Because we are orbiting just as quickly.

That's why we can't feel it. Everything on Earth—cheetahs, trees, cheese pizza—is moving at the same speed, so it feels like our planet isn't even moving.

What do you need

to get a wormhole working?

A very, very hungry worm.

If that doesn't work, a shovel. But you'd be digging forever, because a wormhole isn't an actual hole. A wormhole is a "shortcut" that may exist in space. It's sort of like a super-duper express highway. It might cut your trip from 1,000 years to two years. Some scientists think wormholes develop from forces yet to be discovered. Others argue that they don't exist, because they go against the fundamental principles of physics.

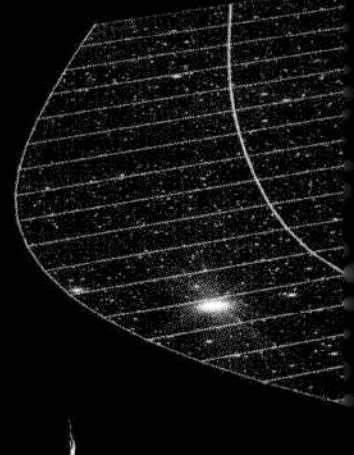

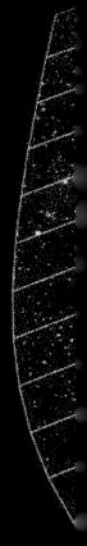

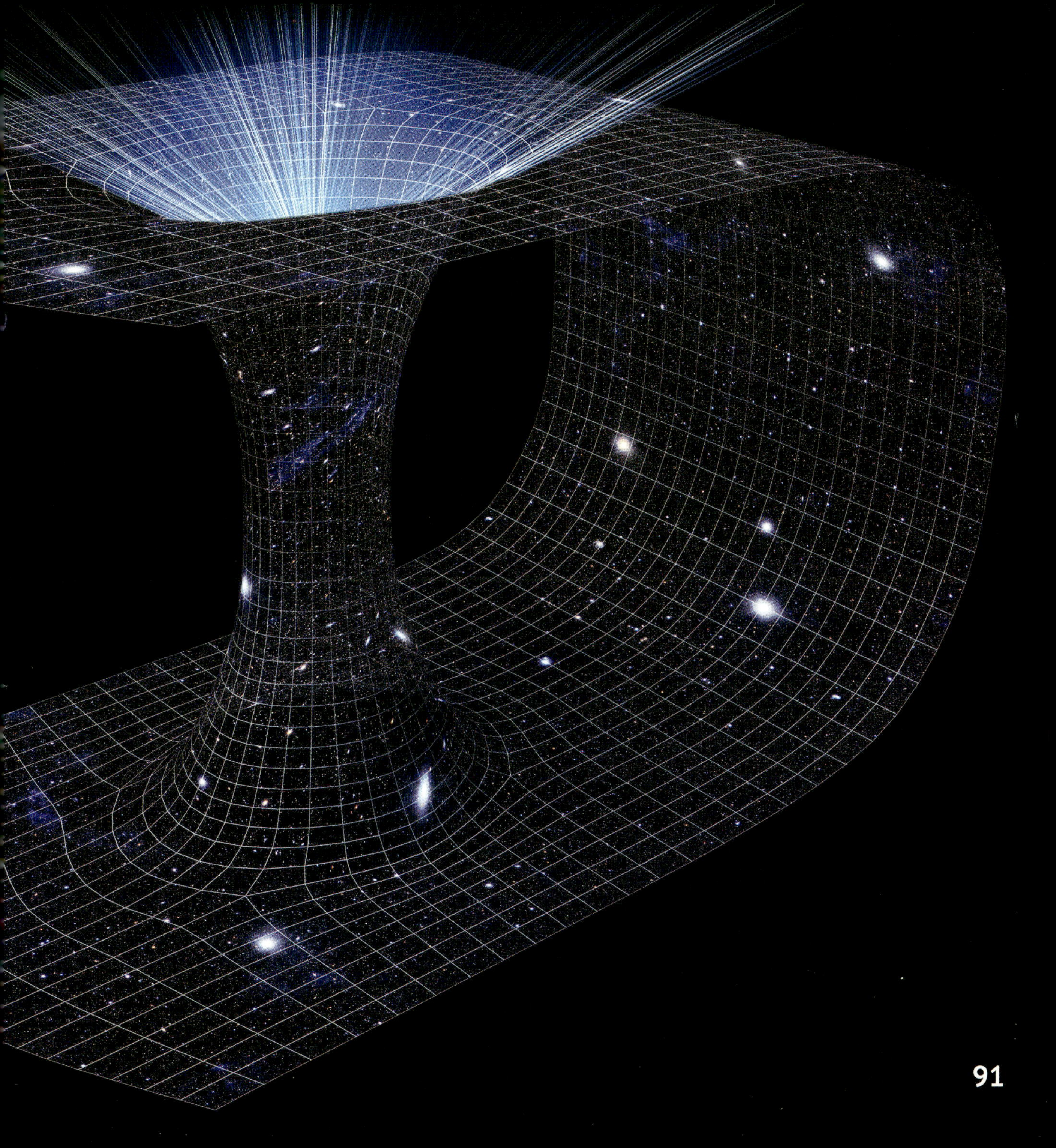

How many people would it take to fill the hole in the galaxy?

Well, we'll never really know.

The center of the galaxy is a huge black hole. When objects fall into a black hole, they disappear forever. They cannot be filled up!

World Book, Inc.
180 North LaSalle Street
Suite 900
Chicago, Illinois 60601
USA

For information about other "Answer Me This, World Book" titles, as well as other World Book print and digital publications, please go to www.worldbook.com.

For information about other World Book publications, call 1-800-WORLDBK (967-5325).

For information about sales to schools and libraries, call 1-800-975-3250 (United States) or 1-800-837-5365 (Canada).

Library of Congress Cataloging-in-Publication Data for this volume has been applied for.

Answer Me This, World Book
ISBN: 978-0-7166-3821-6 (set, hc.)

Is the Milky Way made out of milk?
World Book answers your questions about outer space
ISBN: 978-0-7166-3824-7 (hc.)

Also available as:
ISBN: 978-0-7166-3834-6 (e-book)

Printed in China by RR Donnelley,
Guangdong Province
1st printing July 2019

Acknowledgments

Cover © Denis Belitsky, Shutterstock; © Joy Image/Shutterstock; © Frimu Films/Shutterstock
3-95 © Shutterstock

Staff